DECISION TIME: How Strength–Based Decision Making Changes Everything

STONE LOVE

STONEOLOGYS
BOOKS
SAN FRANCSICO, CALIFORNIA

DECISION TIME: How Strength–Based Decision Making Changes Everything

Copyright © 2015 by Stone Love

ISBN: 978-0-578-14959-251700

ISBN-13:9-780578-149592

Printed in the United States of America

Dearest OnShawn,

You helped to light my way. I'm forever grateful for your presence and grace. I recognize much of myself in you. Thank You!

I love You.

Always,

Stone Love

TESTIMONIALS

In this enlightened narrative Stone shows us from her perspective that our best lessons are gained through our experience. Exceptional Read!

--Dr. Thomas Powers
Board Certified Psychiatrist and is the Medical Director of
Eden Medical Center's Psychiatric Services

◆◆◆◆

My appreciation for letting me read your forward to your book soon to be published.

I have traveled to Tibet, India, Nepal and other spiritual cities and countries and have spoken and listened to many spiritual and holy men and just absorbing their views of life. I find that your book, according to your forward, will merge the person we are now with the spirit within all of us. Your guidelines you have written is in basic plain English that can be understood by any basic reader. I find that there is no need to "read between the lines" to understand the message in your book. Looking forward to your published book.

--Respectfully, Daniel Gan, D.D.S."

◆◆◆◆

Stone Love invites the reader to challenge the mire of fear-based decision-making by first clarifying one's thoughts through a 7 pillar step process. By aligning with one's personal truths, the reader evokes strength-based decisions by realizing the 'power of choice' impacts. A remarkable and carefully thought through work!

--Elaine Fellows MFT

◆◆◆◆

Stone Love is exceptional...Her passion shines through each thought and provides a personal perspective towards making difficult life choices manageable. Great Read!

--Kelly Goins, MBA
Nugenuity Marketing Consultants

i

DEDICATION FROM MY HEART

Forever grateful to my lovely,
strong and dedicated mom
Ms. Virgean Bush
1941~2005.

My mother said yes to my life with hers. I heard her praying this prayer since I was a little girl, "Lord, please let me stay here long enough to see my two babies grow to take care of themselves." God answered her prayer with more than she could ever imagine. She moved from Shreveport, far from everything she new and loved to give her two daughters a better life. We settled in San Francisco, just the three of us. My mom, my sister and I.

Ms. Virgean Bush lived to see many more blessing along with her two daughters growing to independent and loving women. She was able to see her two daughters and her son-in-laws raise 11 grandchildren. They gave her 6 great grand children before she transitioned into her spiritual glory. We were both grandmothers the morning she died, I was thankful. My mom was able to share her love 3 generations wide. There have been 9 more children born since my mom's passing. I see her in the eyes of each of them. My mom's legacy of love continues.

There is a blessing in the mourning. As a grieving daughter, I felt closer to her after she transitioned into my spiritual mother. I was able to speak to her without interruption. Sobbing myself to sleep, I felt understood even though we couldn't speak. I shared things with her soul that I didn't have the heart to tell her when she was alive.

She comforted me in my dreams. She promised to never leave me. I accepted her promise.

The stone in my heart begin to soften and feel love again. As the light came through each morning, I could feel her blessing.

This is what I have grown to know, I have never been separated from her presence. I can access her counsel through my conscience. When I find myself sitting just like she used to, that's when I know she's sitting with me. Everyone always told us we looked just alike. I never saw it until after she was gone. Now, when I look in the mirror there she is.

No one told me, nor did I expect to see her everywhere every day. I am thankful for her spiritual omnipresence in our lives.

My mother's love will always be.

ACKNOWLEDGMENTS

I've had access to some of the best mentors and top coaches. There is one mentor, Nora Profit that has had a life long impact on my writing. Learning how to think about writing, and the importance of word selection has enhanced my communication skills. This knowledge was a shift in my thinking. My speaking is more concise and impactful.

Learning to write a book is more than typing what you have to say and choosing a dazzling book cover. I learned writing is a craft. You must learn how to do it effectively. 'It's about what the reader needs to know.'

I can now write from the readers chair and not the author chair.

I'm grateful to Nora Profit, Founder of The Writing Loft.

Nora is an award-winning journalist, feature writer, columnist, and author.

www.thewritingloft.com

FOREWORD

Just like there are Seven Wonders of the Ancient World, there are seven decision-making techniques we could all learn from.

My good friend Stone Love, shares these seven points in the pages of this book aptly titled "The Seven Pillars of Strength-Based Decisions," which many should find helpful as they engage in their daily lives. I couldn't agree with her more when she says our decisions not only shape our experiences, they also shape the outcomes of our lives.

Whether we are young, old, single, married, a business leader or a stay-at-home mom, there always seems to be a decision to be made. What should I make for dinner? Should I make a financial investment in a stock option? Or, should I even start a business? Sell my business? Have another child, or get a divorce? The list is endless as is the decision-making crossroads we all face, and being positive is one of the best things we can do when we try to make life's choices.

I have had to make some hard choices and decisions over the years, but rather look at these decision-making times in a negative light; I chose, to see through the eyes of gratitude. I choose to see the gifts and lessons in all of the path I walk. Hence CHOOSE! How we engage life is all a matter of perspective. Choice is an attitude and creates our altitude for our successes in life.

From how we engage ourselves in the morning, to when we look in the mirror, to how we interact with others in our home, to how we treat others we work with, is all determined by how we choose to look, act and move.

Everything that you have in your life right now is a direct result of your choices. If you want something different, choose something different. It sounds so simple and yet we can make it be so complex. And what is success anyways? Is it really about money? Sure, money helps. Or, is success more about the awards you win or the recognitions that you get? Life success is about leading and directing your life so you enjoy more of the journey.

Success is truly living a pre-filled life moment by moment by moment. Every choice that you make in the now, changes the now, which changes your future outcome.

You are meant to serve with your gifts and talents; you were born to be happy, be fulfilled, and enjoy the soul journey of all that this life has to offer. Create your own destiny, it is your life and you are meant to play larger than life. Remember: When one light shines, darkness no longer exists and when we all light our candles and shine brilliantly, the world can't help but shine.

Shellie Hunt
CEO/Owner

Success is by Design LLC
www.successisbydesign.com
The Women of Global Change
www.thewomenofglobalchange.com
Phoenix Flight Entertainment
"ReMake MY Life" LLC
www.remakemylife.com
Phoenix Flight Productions LLC
A Full Film Service Company

I decided to think, dream, say and act as if I have the courage to decide and I continue to.
"Decide it IS and so it will BE."

-Stone Love

DECISION TIME: HOW MAKING A STRENGTH-BASED DECISION CHANGES EVERYTHING

"I am not a product of my circumstances. I am a product of my decisions."
~ Stephen Covey

There are seven pillars essential for making strength-based decisions, pillars necessary for laying the foundation for acquiring skills that lead to a life of contentment, pleasure, happiness, and joy. Decision Time not only introduces you to those pillars, it explains them and shows you how to make them a part of your life.

There is a force within us that energetically calls us to recognize the greatness within us—a force that begs us to be who we are and to live the life we were intended to live. We have all experienced the gentle nudges of an energetic invitation to re-evaluate how you will handle life events, and how you will re-evaluate your own self-worth. It is up to you to accept the invitations put to you or not. The ability to exercise strength-based decision-making is one such energetic invitation your spirit holds out to you to embrace. It is an invitation to clear the blocks and conflicts that show up through insecurities, difficult situations, and the negative influences that often times dominate our lives. Instead of being bothered by, frustrated with, or made uncomfortable by what has happened in our lives, we can limit such instances by becoming familiar with, and aligning ourselves with, the concepts of strength-based decision making.

Now is the time to look at every situation in your life as an energetic invitation to clear away negative energy and a recurring change your focus giving you the opportunity to change the typical "what-will-happen-always-happens" to a self-initiated "what-I-decide-will-happen-will-happen."

Energetic invitations bid us to ignore the internal forces that give attention to the negative influences of past events and current misconceptions. Now is the time to change your focus and give yourself the opportunity to be in complete command of the direction of your life. Exercise the principles of strength-based determinations and take the initiative to participate in strength-based thinking that will enable you to take charge of your life. It will enable you to create a comfortable, positive environment in which you can thrive. Strength-based determination is a chance to react in new ways to the things that seemingly never change—the things that will dull your existence. It is possible to change your perspective and truly improve your lot by understanding the power of making every decision with strength, authority, and control.

It will take an honest effort to change the way you see things and open to releasing the part you play when interacting with everyone and everything around you. However, it is not impossible and you can do it. You see, we are not responsible for the bad things that have happened to us over which we have had no control. But we are responsible for what we do today. We are the product of each and every decision we make today and in the future. We are the masters of our own destiny and the captain of our own soul. Strength-based decision-making assures that we will be able to make decisions and choices we truly want to make and have the outcomes we truly want to happen.

The one nemesis to strength-based decision-making is fear—fear that forces compromised choices. It is emotional pain, the strong influence of others, and a fear of all kinds that leave us open to making decisions based on false realities, false belief systems, imagined external controls, and dread. Fear-based decisions rob us of clarity, self-preservation, and a life we were never intended to live.

It is imperative to know that the pillars of strength-based decision making laid out in this book, are parts of an integrated whole that can't be separated; each pillar relies on the functioning of the other. It is therefore important to practice each pillar in conjunction with the others. Make the practice of strength-based decision-making a interconnected exercise with the intended result of taking control of who you really are. Claim the peace that comes with a self-directed life of independence, peace, and personal accountability.

There is greatness in each of us. We should never hesitate to recognize it. We should never be afraid to name it and claim it for ourselves. It is a strange thing that we seldom fail to recognize the brilliance, ability, and the potential of others, but seldom see or accept it in ourselves. We marvel at those we believe are living their best lives and often think such a life is beyond our reach. We fail to notice the energetic invitation our own spirits call for us to declare our brilliance and the power we already possess to orchestrate the kind of life we want to live.

The moment we are faced with a decision, we should consider the outside influences swirling around in our lives at the time. We should recognize what elements are actually suggesting a particular course of action and which emotions are having the strongest affect on us. We should consider whether one, or all, of those influences have our best interest at heart.

When Shania was faced unexpectedly with having to move in 30 days, several things came to mind: her daughter's school, her mother's health, her job, the impact on her budget, and on and on. She gave all those thoughts priority in her thinking but little or no consideration to how her decisions would affect her emotionally and spiritually. She failed to realize that making her best decision was not a question of just choosing what seems to be a best option out of many. Shania had to learn the difference between what the reality of an outcome would be instead of the outcome she hoped would be. The "best" choice in any situation is not which choice has the strongest emotional pull; or the one other people believe is the most logical; or the one that appears to be the most spiritual; or the one we think is the "best" choice for everyone involved. Decision-making is much more than that. It can be something stronger and more reliable. It is making decisions you know you are making from a position of strength. A decision is "best" when it takes into account all the elements that signal the right way for you, not anyone else. Decisions made from strength are decisions that can be considered your "best" decision.

STRENGTH-BASED DECISIONS: THE FOUNDATION

To make strength-based decisions, first take a look at your current decision patterns. Ask yourself why you revert to a pattern regardless of the situation. A decision pattern is a repeated way of acting regardless of a given situation. If you have a pattern of decision-behaviors that fail to pay attention to how a decision nourishes your life, then it will support a bad decision over and over again. What this means, is that we have to be mindful of whether we make decisions out of fear and revert to a seemingly safe pattern or whether we have properly evaluated options that are best for the peace and comfort of our life.

If we are paying attention to what is motivating us, we can understand where things begin and where they have the potential to end up. Without paying attention to our lives and our experiences, we lose the calmness that provides balance and a sense of control and safety. Without paying attention to the underlying patterns of the behaviors that create and drive our lives, we will end up constantly spinning in circles repeating the life experiences we don't want.

Once you know yourself, your behavior patterns will change. It is no secret that we pick up scripted behavior patterns during our journey through life—some are good and some are bad. We have the power to choose which of those patterns enhance our lives and which of those patterns tend to destroy our lives and our ability to have positive experiences. There is one thing to note however, once you decide to change your behavior patterns, you will inevitably meet with strong resistance. It will be as though forces are fighting against you. People who know you will feel uncomfortable with the new you and may unconsciously work against any changes. Be alert and maintain your determination and resolve in spite of the resistance. Remain steadfast in your new behaviors and resistance will fade.

Next, take into consideration the extent to which you have been willing to surrender to manipulation particularly in the face of fear. You must be adamant that you will make strength-based decisions rather than decisions that are fear-based. When faced with a decision—any decision—strength dies when fear reigns. Take a good look at every situation you've encountered and ask yourself if fear is an element that has been running your life.

Fear comes in multiple forms. It can manifest itself as an internal bias preventing personal growth. It can come in the form of emotional pain leaving you open to making decisions that are both powerless and destructive. Poor thinking practices can translate into decisions made out of fear.

Failure to follow any of the steps discussed in this book can translate into decisions that fail to reflect the person you are inside. If you make decisions inconsistent with your inner spirit, it will not only thwart your intentions, it will stunt the person you are on the inside.

THE POWER OF THOUGHT

It is important for you to acknowledge the incredible power of thought. Before you begin your journey through the steps of strength-based decision-making, you must first take into consideration the power thinking has and how it affects every decision you will make now and in the future.

Affective and powerful thinking comes from knowing that thoughts—thoughts of all kinds—have power. If you fail to recognize the power of your thoughts, you will negate an important source of your strength and ability to discern truth. Some thoughts are beneficial to your life and others are destructive. Some are lies you've been fed over the years, others are lies you've told yourself—lies about your abilities and your potential.

You may be under the impression that you can't control what you think. You may believe that no matter what you tell yourself you can't change what you are thinking or how you feel about those thoughts. But you would be wrong. People often think they aren't even sure from where a thought has come. However, the truth is that you are the author of your thoughts. You can control what you think and how you feel about everything you think.

Clear thinking is also the key to physical and spiritual health. Your thoughts are so powerful that they can be responsible for psychological and physical responses that have nothing to do with any current situation or circumstance at hand. Thoughts can cause palpitations, high blood pressure, urges to overeat, emotional spending, and even an urge toward emotional dating. It is your willingness to participate in the clear-cut process of evaluating the quality of your thoughts that will allow you to make enlightened decisions. When your thoughts are under control, your judgments are always of a higher quality.

Your thoughts are your own and you, and only you, can manage them to your benefit. When you acknowledge that you are the author of your thoughts and that those thoughts have the power to affect your life, then you will gain the power necessary to control both your present circumstance and your future. You will be able to dictate your destiny. Once you become comfortable with the idea that you can control your thinking, you will have obtained the foundation upon which the principles of *Decision Time* are built. You can go from powerless to powerful in an instant. You will be sure that when there is a decision to be made, you are making the right one. Below are examples of life-changing thoughts and how changing one's thinking has the power to change one's circumstance.

"I've been a broken woman since my husband left."
Simply change that to, "It is time to break out of these old married clothes and shop for new pieces that represent me."
"I can't stand the thought of never seeing my mother again."
Change that to, "I have never been separated from my mother. When I am quiet, I can hear her laughter. When I am loud, I can hear her voice emanating from my words."

So, determine if you are participating in thoughts that are painful and restrictive. If so, change those thoughts to thoughts that redefine the event. A change in your thought patterns will bring to light any debilitating illusions you may have. It will also break the shackles restricting your growth and the recognition of future possibilities. There is a thin line between a catastrophic thought and a euphoric thought. Your life is influenced by the way you think and poor thinking expresses itself in future events. Poor thinking and perpetually giving in to negative illusions will cause the perpetuation of an unwanted existence and an unhealthy emotional state. This is your challenge: redefine your thinking right now.

Anyone who fails to recognize that thoughts are the reason

for embedded feelings of discontentment, also fail to realize that negative thinking is a nemesis. Thought has the power to continually cause you to relive negative events and the result of poor decisions. As a result, those negative events and choices then become a recurring theme in your life; same results, different actors. It will be the same old story over and over again.

Change your thinking and you will create more positive experiences for yourself. If you immerse yourself in self-pity, you will be miserable. If you continually live in the past, you will never have a future. If you continuously indulge in the negative, it will manifest itself in your body. Your body responds physiologically to your thoughts and your words, so control what you say and what you think. Make your mind the guardian of your future. The power thoughts have is not new information, but you can practice positive thinking like it is new. So, from this day forward, evaluate your thoughts. Ask yourself if they are true and if they are consistent with whom you are. Ask yourself if your thoughts allow you to be intimidated and force you to give your power away.

Poor thinking is a major obstacle to real problem solving and strength-based decision making. It is therefore important to know that poor thinking can result in the following negative reactions, all of which affect the quality of your life.

Doubt:

Doubt is disabling. If you fail to take control of vacillating thinking and allow doubt in it will invade your mind, and cripple the characteristic benefits that come from an effective thought process.

As horrible as doubt can be, it is easily thwarted. Doubt is merely the result of low self-esteem, a lack of confidence in your God-given abilities, and an acceptance of a false set of information. Doubt, when left unchecked, becomes a self-fulfilling prophecy. Doubters make decisions from of a state of confusion and insecurity. People who doubt themselves are never sure what to do or how to do it. They become so ruled by insecurity that it makes them vulnerable to the whims of anyone who desires to insinuate themselves into the doubter's life.

Anxiety:

Anxiety, like doubt, can be controlled and eliminated. It is the control of anxiety that is indispensible to making calm and stress-free decisions. Unrealistic and anxious feelings not only affect your sound decision-making ability, it also affects your stress level and ultimately your health. Decisions that are not stress-free are made under duress and never result in the outcomes we really want for ourselves.

It is easy to detect when you are anxious or when you are surrendering to anxiety. When your insides are in turmoil, uneasy, or are in a state of confusion, you are in the throws of anxiety. There is a strong feeling of dread over something that may or may not happen. There is a strong uneasiness when asked to do something incompatible with our life-goals or desires.

Anxiety is a strong and unpleasant feeling of fear, worry, and uneasiness. It often causes us to become unfocused and consequently overreact to situations without direction or purpose. Anxiety causes muscular tension, restlessness, fatigue, and problems concentrating.

Illusions:

Illusions are the false understanding of circumstances and/or information that is mistaken for truth. It is a strong misconception of how things really are.

It is a misinterpretation or misunderstanding of information you were given as a child—information you may be including in your current life just because of how you perceive events in your past. Our illusion of what truth is often comes from information gleaned from others or our imagination. It's based on information and ideas gleaned from partial information. Such reliance on incorrect information often causes us to make decisions that can't possibly serve us for the better.

Illusions are also often at the core of how we determine our self-worth. We draw vivid conclusions based on scanty sketches of what we believe and what has been implanted in our minds. We accept false beliefs about our character, self-worth, and status garnered from our race, economic status, and/or gender. Most of what we believe, and have operated on, has often been a series of half-truths, complete falsehoods, or incorrect conclusions. There are sometimes things that were true in the past, but are not even close to being true today. The nearest escape from the danger and distress of bad information is your determination to acknowledge truth and change your belief system. Doing that, will eventually change how you think and perceive everything. You will soon become proficient at recognizing what beliefs are illusions and which ones are actually true.

It is important to re-evaluate what things you believe to be true for one important reason: believing an illusion can cause havoc in your life now and in the future. Ask yourself what illusions you are currently operating under. Take time to draw parallels between the kinds of thinking you may have adopted as a child and the kinds of thinking you are relying on as an adult. Recognize where false thinking patterns crop up in your adult life and then question their authenticity.

Remember, whatever your story, you are not your story. I repeat, you are not your story. You are not your past. The reality is that there is only today. The past is gone and the future hasn't happened yet. The events that have happened in your life do not define you neither do they diminish you. They strengthen you and give you permission to be who you have always wanted to be. Change your definition of yourself and the events in your life will change. When you think about your story—or tell it to others—make sure it is your view of the story and not the handed-down view of others. It is your view of who you are that determines the impact of your experiences as well as how others will perceive you. Change your definition of painful and restrictive thoughts and you will change who you are for the better.

Discontentment:

Discontentment comes from harboring ideas and perceptions that are not true of you. They are intrusive and harmful ideas that disrupt your peace of mind. Refuse to give your contentment away, and in a calm manner, opt for clear unbiased thinking. You lose your contented self—the force that brings peace—when you fail to look at circumstances with clarity. To obtain clarity on any level means you have to look at things the way they really are, not the way you wish them to be. Take your time. Look at things calmly. You can obtain and maintain contentment when you evaluate whether your behaviors and circumstances are beneficial to you. If anything makes you feel uncomfortable, it is the beginning of a loss of contentment. A refusal to accept reality can keep you in a state of denial, grief, and confusion, all of which are destructive to your ability to be content.

Contentment is quiet, peaceful, self-assured, and pleased with the way things are for now. It does not focus on what you have or don't have. Rather, it focuses on just being in a state of satisfaction. We choose whether we are happy or unhappy, choose to be happy.

Although you may have thought—as many people do—that happiness comes from being rich or beautiful or living a stress-free life. The reality is that people who have wealth, beauty, or appear to be less stressed, are not any happier on average than those who don't enjoy those blessings.

People who are happy seem to know intuitively that their happiness is the sum total of their life choices. That is why making decisions supported by strength are built on the following intentions and the foundations for a contented life:

- Devotion of time to family and friends.
- Appreciation for what one already has.
- Maintaining an optimistic outlook regardless of circumstance.
- Having a sense of purpose.
- Living in the moment—not the past or the future.

If you give attention to developing a culture of contentment that will preserve your spiritual wealth, it will be an effort that pays off now and in the future. Focus on what brightens your day and leave the negativity to others. Grant yourself a lifetime of permission to have spiritual wealth, longevity, and health.

Follow the suggestions below:

- Remove toxic behaviors from your life, particularly those around finances.
- Identify toxic people and refuse to relinquish your contentment to them.
- Eliminate small stressors. You've heard the saying, "Choose your battles." You can't win every battle, but you can win the war. Take author Richard Carlson's advice and "Don't sweat the small stuff".
- Be open to growth. Nothing stays the same and neither should you. Anything that isn't growing is on its way to rotting. Life is about seasons; and seasons change.

Recognize that growth involves change.
- Give to others with grace. It is a blessing to give without expecting a return on kindness. If you give with the expectation of reward, then your giving is merely a loan for which the 'interest' should be stated up front.
- In all things, be thankful. Thankfulness is what makes us fruitful. Thankfulness is the foundation upon which contentment is built.

Above all things, contentment requires that you free your self of regret, disappointment, and hurt feelings. Forgive yourself and forgive others. It is impossible to make the right choice each and every time you make a decision. But, as you get to know yourself, and your wants and needs, you will begin to make better and better choices. Any decisions you have made in the past and consider wrong, know that it was the best decision you were capable of making at the time. You will make better decisions as you learn more about yourself and the reality of your past. You will make better decisions when you adopt a fearless intention to have a positive future. Maya Angelou once said, "When you know better, you do better." Forgive yourself for the past and resolve to live life anew.

"You may not be able to control all the events that happen to you," Angelou says, "but you can decide not to be reduced by them."

If you actively look for the blessing in all things, you will learn how to affectively show up in your own life. You will learn to make decisions that you not only consider to be right, but they will be decisions that serve your life's goals and direction.

Be optimistic. Believe the answers you need are already within your grasp. When you give yourself the benefit of the doubt, you allow solutions to come to your mind. There is a scientific benefit in assuming success and being positive about your existence in this world. Assuming success energizes the possibilities of your success. Own the power of your presence in this world, Admit the reality that you are unique, valuable, and prized.

Lack of Concentration:

If you are unable to concentrate, you will not have the ability for rational and concrete evaluation. Concentration is an essential tool for assessing and gauging any situation or problem. To effectively solve a problem you must be able to concentrate on the problem. Take your time to initiate a calm consideration of the facts. You must also be able to concentrate long enough to compartmentalize each issue. Set each issue or idea apart until you can effectively convey those ideas in a timely manner to yourself first, and to others later. Stay focused on your strengths. Don't be intimidated. If you are willing to learn new things, it will prevent you from being intimidated. Decide if you are submitting to intimidation or have agreed to that intimidation willingly. The weight of intimidation will most certainly destroy your concentration and your focus.

Given the information we've just discussed, it is now your responsibility to analyze your ability to concentrate. A wandering mind will lead to procrastination especially when an issue is urgent or important. Know that procrastination is just a substitute for taking your time to concentrate on an issue at hand. Procrastination does not change or delay the outcome of a situation; it only takes the issue out of your control and puts it in the hand of someone else. Since questions or issues never remain undecided, procrastination serves no purpose.

In order to concentrate, make it a rule to sit down, quiet yourself and find a place where you can think. Then force yourself to focus. Your failure to concentrate is also a failure to control your thinking. Trust yourself. When you have confidence in your ability to make good decisions, your lack of concentration will disappear. People often have negative thoughts they fail to acknowledge and it is those thoughts that convince them they are unable to tackle a problem. Negativity makes it difficult to concentrate. It is a preprograming of your thinking that won't allow new thinking or possibility thinking. Take some time to evaluate why you can't concentrate and then tackle whatever you encounter.

Failure to Recognize Choice:

One of the most amazing faculties we have is our power to choose. Regardless of what you may think or what others may have said, we do have the power of choice. Everything is a choice and you are the one to decide. You can decide how you feel about a situation or event. You can decide whether you will participate or not. You can decide not to accept anything that makes you feel less-than. You decide your future, all of it.

You can choose the lifestyle you want, your religious affiliation and who you decide to marry. Take hold of this power already within your grasp, and control your now and your later. The only thing that keeps you from claiming this power with passion and enthusiasm is fear. We will deal with this life-destroying phantom later in the book. For now, the foundation for being all you can be is to work all the steps of strength-based decision-making.

Lack of Emotional Awareness:

Emotional awareness is the ability to identify and manage your own emotions and the emotions of others. It is also the ability to use emotions to enhance your thinking and dictate how they will benefit your life. Emotional awareness is not doing away your emotions or pretending a lack of emotion. It is the ability to use your emotions to enhance your life, your responses, and your decisions.

It is important to recognize what emotions you are having,

and when and why. Emotional awareness involves knowing what triggers an emotional response and why you react as you do. Emotions aren't something to dismiss lightly. It behooves you to think them through. See if you can find connections between your feelings and the other times you may have felt that same way. Ask yourself, "When have I felt like this before?" You may find that your current emotion is an autonomic response to a specific situation or an incident in your past. When you feel something that strikes you in a peculiar way ask, "What do I really think about that?" Once you answer that question, you will understand the emotion and how to use it to your benefit. You can decide to deal with the situation in a way that benefits you rather than in a way that brings you to a stand still.

There will be times when you experience conflicting emotions. This is normal. Your job is to sort out those emotions and listen to each one as though you were listening to the witnesses in a court case. Gather all the facts you can and then come to an un-emotional verdict. You will then be able to figure out why you are experiencing those emotions and what to do about them.

It is also important to listen to your body when you are experiencing an emotion. Paying attention to how you are feeling will allow you to process the 'why' of an emotion and use your powers of reason to evaluate them. If you don't know how you are feeling at a particular moment, ask someone you trust to help you. There are others who know you and may know exactly what you are feeling and why.

After you have thoroughly looked inward at the cause of your emotion, look outward. There may be an environmental cause as to why you are feeling as you do. There may be one particular person who is adept at pushing your buttons or a location that makes you feel uncomfortable. These are emotions you can change in an instant. Avoid the offending location and don't allow the button-pushing person to have power over you. Enhance the frequency of environmental forces that result in positive emotions.

HOW TO MAKE STRENGTH-BASED DECISIONS AND CHANGE YOUR LIFE FOREVER:

Strength-based decisions are the underpinning of a successful life. It is the foundation that puts control of your circumstance back into your hands. Once we become adults, everything that happens in our lives is directly linked to the decisions we make. So how and why you make decisions will determine the success or failure of your life. Stephen Covey urges us to remember that we are not the product of our circumstances we are however the result of all the decisions we've made throughout our life.

Today will be a new day when you discover how to take control of your life by taking control of the decisions you make. Today is the day to learn that you can change your life and your circumstance by changing the method you use for making your decisions. Remember, you are the result of the decisions you make and those decisions will ultimately create your life experiences. It is not only important to make 'relevant-to-your-life' decisions, it is important to make decisions built on the foundation of your personal strengths.

Learning to make strength-based decisions is important because it will:
- Allow you to decide how you will experience the memories of past events now that you are safe and free to make your own decisions.
- Give you the tools to mentally move from victimhood.
- Allow you to discover who *you* really are—the *'you'* you've always wanted to be, but weren't sure you were.
- Allow you to discover what you really want out of life and focus on getting it.

- Show you how to make decisions that are best for you in the midst of the myriad of influences that invade your thinking.
- Show you how to course-correct your journey and aim in which direction you really want to go.
- Help you feel safe, free, and comfortable to making decisions aligned with whom you are on the inside and project on the outside.

Success is most often the result of wisdom, good judgment, and good decision-making. However, in order to know if a decision is right for you, it must be made from a position of strength. Failing to know who you are at your deepest level, or failing to know what you really want, is the enemy of strength-based decision making.

Fear and intimidation is a major factor that makes strength-based decisions impossible. Fear and intimidation rob you of who you are and place your wants, desires and needs so far at the bottom of the list that they are never considered. Fear and intimidation ensures that there will never be any input from you.

Intimidation, like fear, comes in many forms. It comes in so many forms that it is often disguised as something as harmless as help—help that appears to be practical and reasonable, but is nothing more than a mild form of manipulation. The manipulative form of intimidation puts the recipient in a position difficult to escape. It creates a situation of forced trust and makes the recipient afraid to disagree with the help or advice for fear of being labeled as ungrateful or unappreciative. Gratefulness and appreciation however have nothing to do with accepting or rejecting someone's help. You can appreciate the fact they thought of you and were concerned, but whether you take their advice or not does not factor into things. If the person makes the acceptance of their help or advice mandatory then it isn't help at all, it is manipulation. Help is only help, when or if, you can use it. Help is not help if it has a mandatory condition that you use it.

Fear on the other hand, is often the result of the influences and experiences of past events. We tend to put a tremendous amount of importance on past events believing that such experiences are a sure guide to how to handle future events. However, what you believe about a past event may not be true, or you may not have a clear memory of the facts. You may fear the recurrence of a situation without fully understanding the corollaries of it. Or, you may believe the experience was positively handled without being privileged to the negative ramifications that resulted later. You may have been too young to understand and not party to all the facts. Challenge your memories. Seek to understand events by how they present themselves today.

What happened in the past is certainly of great benefit to your accumulation of experiential wisdom. You can learn more about yourself and your behaviors by analyzing past events. But using past events as an indisputable guide to current situations without evaluation and reasoning is not wise. Each past event has a different and unique lesson to teach. It is your job to ascertain what that lesson is and how—if it does—aid in making a decision today.

In other words, fear and unknowing can cause you to make poor decisions. If fear is motivating a judgment of any kind, re-evaluate the fear and place it in the light of reason. Ask what it is you actually fear and whether that fear is justified. Fear should never be a motive for making a decision or evaluating a situation. Use clear thinking as the drive for making a decision (see the section on "The Power of Thought" p. 7).

The most powerful of all the fears is the fear of criticism.

People often allow friends, relatives, and the public at large to so influence them that they cannot live their lives for fear of criticism. It is a fear of being criticized for your choices, opinions, thoughts, and beliefs that can keep you from moving forward. Fear of criticism rests in your subconscious mind where its powerful presence is not always recognized. It is this fear that not only wrecks your ability to make conscientious decisions, but rules the quality of your life.

Criticism is nothing more than a form of manipulation and intimidation. It creates a habit of compromising your will and desires for the will and desires of someone else. It is wishing for things to be a certain way instead of insisting on making them the way you want.

It may be hard to hear, but it boils down to this: a fear of criticism is a lack of drive and ambition on your part. It is reaching for short cuts instead of facing life squarely and demanding that you get what you want and need. Remember you think, believe, and decide is just as valid as the thoughts and feelings of anyone else.

When you are unable to clearly define and comfortably know what you want to yourself, it is quite possible that you are dealing with a fear of criticism. This fear causes procrastination on your part because any decisions are not your own. Procrastination becomes a fallback position followed by an array of excuses that are nothing more than weak substitutes for saying no. Instead of opting for doing things to make your own life shine, fear-victims search for short cuts they believe will please others instead of themselves.

Fear-driven individuals don't take chances. They don't take chances simply because they are afraid they will be criticized. A life afraid makes it almost impossible to make concrete plans or design a life you want simply because if you did make plans for your life, someone might not approve. Manipulators get to live the lives they want, but you don't. Instead, you live their idea of what your life should be. Trace your alibis and excuses back to their origins and you will find a fear of criticism. Fear-driven individuals seldom set high goals for themselves or follow through on selected careers because they fear the criticism of relatives and friends who may say something like, "Don't aim so high. People will think you are proud and conceited".

That one sentence is enough for some people to abandon a life-long dream or ambition. Huge numbers of people make mistakes and continue to endure those mistakes because they are too afraid change—even if it's a change for the better. Those people go through life miserable and unhappy because they fear the criticism they may have to endure should they choose to correct the mistake.

Tania married Devon to the praises, compliments, and approval of everyone. Devon had the right executive job, made lots of money, and was outrageously handsome. Everyone thought Tania struck gold. The truth was however, Devon was never thoughtful, kind, or respectful. He was self-centered and believed a wife's job was to serve him and him alone. How Tania behaved, what she did, and any decisions she made had to be approved by him.

Tania lived in an expensive house and wore expensive high-fashion clothes; all to Devon's liking and approval. It was a life everyone thought was ideal. And it was ideal to everyone except Tania. Life for Tania was a living hell.

Five years after the marriage, Tania took the time to seriously contemplate her plight. She decided a change was in order. However, her decision to change was met with strong criticism at all fronts. A few friends laid the problem at her doorstep. They warned she wasn't being practical or sensible. They cautioned she would lose her coveted, easy lifestyle, fancy clothes, and comfortable living conditions all because she only thought she was uncomfortable. They suggested that if she tried harder she could change him. They also cautioned that others live with controlling spouses and therefore, she could as well.

Others enlisted fear. They warned of the impending doom she would meet if she divorced. They also articulated what they thought would be her reality: she would have to start over with nothing; she would be a failure and would not be able to come back from that. They expressed how difficult it would be for her to find a job in an already tight market; that she would end up alone; and how impossible it would be for her to make it on her own.

Tania's only choice was to make a decision backed by strength. She followed the principles of strength-based decision making and the first thing she did was change her way of thinking. She decided she could make it on her own if that is what she wanted. She refused to give into fear or allow herself to be manipulated by it. She took time to look at the reality of the problem and decided the input she was getting was not based on facts. The input was nothing more than negative assumptions. She realized the advice she was given was not advice at all, it was intimidation cleverly disguised as help.

Tania knew what she wanted out of life and a lack of freedom was not part of it. She realized she had the strength of her convictions and a belief in herself if she chose to use them. She also realized she had the inner strength to follow through on any decisions designed to better her life and her life only. She believed in her ability to make choices that would elevate what she wanted and needed from life. Knowing herself at a deep level made it possible to ignore the fear of 'what-if' and muster the courage to follow her own intentions.

Anyone who has submitted to the kind of criticism and fear that Tania had to face knows the irreversible damage it can do to ambition and self- reliance. It destroys who you are and dampens your brilliance within. The fear of criticism sometimes appears to be stronger than the desire for a real life, but one's own survival instincts must be strong.

In order to make decisions that serve you and your life goals, you must abandon fear of criticism, fear of failure, and fear of risk. To embark on a journey where decisions enhance your life—ones that are made from a position of power—you have to submit to a thorough concentration on yourself and your needs. You have to commit to in-depth thinking. You have to integrate, live, and work the pillars of strength-based decision-making.

You can test every decision you make against the pillars you learn here in this book. Each concept—each pillar—is an important part of an integrated whole. Each strength-based decision pillar serves to establish and maintain a power that enables you to live a life that results in strength-based decision-making. Each pillar will help you lay the foundation on which strong worthwhile decisions are made.

I urge you to learn each concept in turn and then add it to the others as you go. Not one of the concepts can stand alone if you are attempting to make decisions that will enhance your life. Know that each concept—each step you take—promises that you will live the life you have decided you want to live.

"Your past may inform and influence your life,
but your decisions transform your future."

- Stone Love

THE SEVEN PILLARS TO MAKING STRENGTH-BASED DECISIONS

PILLAR NUMBER ONE: PEACE

When attempting to make a decision, ask yourself, "Do you have a peace about it?" If you are toiling over choices and worried about outcomes, then you do not have an inward peace about the decision. The fact of the matter is, that when something is right for you, you'll have peace about it. There will be a calm spirit that comes without effort, question or second-guessing. When something is right for you—and no one else—there will be a peace about it. There will be no question as to what you should do.

If you don't feel peaceful about a choice, then quiet your mind, find a place to be still, mull over your choices, and do nothing until you do have peace. The process of quieting yourself will allow insights to come to mind. It will let your spirit and inner-self have a say. Decisions are hard. They are seldom peaceful in nature. However, it is still important that you have peace about any action you take. Again, ask yourself, "Do I have a peace about it?"

Decision-making is one of those times when your feelings are important. So, look inside yourself and decide whether you have a feeling of calm around a decision. Take into consideration whether you have an inward peace about your decision. Your spirit should be confident and composed. It should be calm regardless of whether others suggest you will regret the decisions or not. Remember, peace of mind is being mentally and spiritually calm, and comfortable with the knowledge and understanding that you can keep your self-strong in the face of opposition, discord, and stress.

If you are unsure of how you are feeling, quiet your mind. Sit silently and empty your mind of thought. Keep everything simple and above all, take your time. There is never a rush to do anything at that very moment. Remember, this is only one decision. Think less about the past or future. Think only of what is at hand. You can't do everything or be everything. Today is different from the past. Let go of bias and expectations. Be still, do nothing. Just employ the power of peace. Listen to your body, to your heart, and to your spirit. Then ask yourself with finality, "Do I have a peace about this?"

Georgina, a single parent and mother of three boys, asked that very question when things became muddled and a decision critical. She was faced with a dramatic decision when her son Daniel was arrested for the third time. Daniel was only fifteen. The school, the Social Services Department, and the police presented options with a strong view of insisted obedience.

The school's therapist thought a woman without a husband or family support was unable to make an effective decision. The solution presented by Social Services was much more than a suggestion. It included a veiled threat to put Daniel in foster care. Both alternatives would not only affect Daniel, but would dramatically affect her entire family. She quieted her mind and began to think. She refused to be manipulated by fear. She took the time to evaluate the reality of the situation and then listened to her intuition. She considered what the outcomes might be and her willingness to participate in those outcomes. She consulted her experiential wisdom, considered strongly what she wanted for her son's life, and looked for a decision that would give her the most peace. She also considered each strength-based pillar in turn and came to the only decision that would uplift her life and the life of her son.

Georgia decided to enlist the help of a private therapist even though the cost would be enormous and the time commitment great. She also enlisted the help of influential black male role models that would give her son a different outlook on life. She then worked diligently and wisely to get the school and social services on her side and accept the decisions she made.

It was Georgia's new ability to think rationally and calmly about her situation that determined her success. Her determination to go in the direction of her wants and needs brought about positive results.

Georgia is proof that we should never let the weight of an issue, or the opinions of others, no matter how powerful, to be the only factor to influence a decision. Georgia decided what she needed and employed the strength of her convictions to make it happen.

PILLAR REFLECTION: PEACE

Think of a time when you allowed disharmony in your life. What caused it?

_____

_____

_____

_____

_____

_____

_____

_____

_____

_____

_____

_____

Action Steps or New Thought Processes: Peace

Due to the consequences of disharmony listed above, what will you do differently?

_____

_____

_____

_____

_____

_____

_____

_____

_____

_____

_____

Please bring your questions about this pillar to Decision Time live event or a complimentary call with Stone Love.

NOTES

NOTES

PILLAR NUMBER TWO: WISDOM

There is always an element of wisdom important to any decision. Decisions are never black or white and they are never clear-cut. After you have determined that you have a feeling of peace with a likely decision, ask yourself, "It is wise for me?" In other words, what is the wisdom of any possible decision from your point of view, your experience, and your current circumstance?

Ask yourself what is the wisdom in it for you, and you alone. What do you believe to be true? Are you succumbing to the subtle influence others may be quietly imposing on you? It is important that you assess and understand the wisdom of your choices so you can apply that information to your decisions. An important part of making a decision with strength is deciding if the decision is wise. Evaluate each decision through your lens only. Then, consider the pros and cons of each decision based on your needs, your experience, your past knowledge, your moral convictions, and—above all—your non-negotiable principles.

Sound judgments are judgments depend on integrating your decisions with the essence of the person you are inside. For that reason, it is important to give credit to your spirit, your feelings, and your intuition. Who you are on the inside is always guiding you with energetic invitations to listen to your inward advice—invitations from your spirit that endeavor to protect you. Your spirit pleads for you to submit to the real you—the one you are inside.

The Importance of Wisdom

It behooves all of us to analyze what wisdom is and how it enables us to live a more productive life. Wisdom is the ability to come to the right understanding of things. Superficial knowledge that considers only what is apparent is not true wisdom. In order to acquire wisdom, you must penetrate the veil of superficial reality down to its core. A child sees the ocean and beach as playful and fun. But an adult recognizes that while the waves lapping against the sand can be playful, the pull of those same waves can be dangerous. Even the sun must be shielded against to avoid sunburn, dehydration, and damage to our eyes. An adult considers the entire reality of any situation. Wisdom dictates that we go beyond a superficial examination of things to be sure our decisions result in the outcome we intend.

Wisdom dictates that we go to the depths with penetrating insight to correctly assess what the underlying truth is in every situation. It is not enough to consider things consciously. We have to consider what our unconscious mind is telling us. Our unconscious mind, our spirit, knows us best.

There are three kinds of wisdom. The first is the wisdom gained by hearing or reading the words of others. The second is intellectual wisdom—using one's reasoning and analytical faculties to determine whether the input we receive is rational and logical.

The third kind of wisdom is experiential wisdom. It is a wisdom manifested within you that is based on past experiences and is therefore beneficial and should be valued. This type of wisdom originates from within the self. Experiential wisdom comes from a real and profound understanding of the impact, results, and sensory input gleaned from experience. Experiential wisdom is the 'decision' to 'apply' those lessons you've learned on a cellular level over time. It is firsthand practical information and therefore the highest level of wisdom you can achieve.

The Value of Experiential Wisdom

Experiential wisdom teaches us that we have to evaluate both our emotions and our thoughts before we act. Experiential wisdom is more than learning from your past or the mistakes of others. It is learning what triggers our emotional responses and our patterns of fear.

Thinking most often serves at the beck and call of emotion, so it is both emotion and thought patterns that must be controlled. Failure to heed this information often results in the loss of friendships and situations that are important. It was a neglect of this that Salome, a businesswoman and writer, gleaned as experiential wisdom in an encounter with her publisher.

Salome had a close relationship with her publisher and was glad to have such a person on her team. She trusted this woman to evaluate her manuscript and make changes at her discretion. Salome had no doubt about the integrity, skill, and ability of this publisher, but an innate fear crept into her thinking every time she considered what may or may not happen. Salome's fear raised its head so often that the publisher threatened to quit the project on the spot. Her extensive requests for proof of skill angered the publisher and put the project in jeopardy. Salome had no one else she trusted and no other person she could rely on to accomplish the task, but she still allowed unreasonable fear and emotion to dictate her behavior.

In a final effort to quell her fear, Salome took a long look at what was actually operating in her mind. She realized that her fear was unfounded. She was risking an important relationship without good reason. She knew she was merely operating on emotion. Evaluating her fear and emotion against reality added to Salome's emotional maturity and experiential wisdom.

Salome learned how every experience adds to our ability to train our thinking and add to our evolution into total emotional maturity. Emotional maturity provides the necessary foundation for an essential leap from thought to wisdom. Knowing the truth and getting comfortable with it, is a monumental step to understanding yourself.

Re-educate yourself about how mature thinking is done (see the section on "The Power of Thought", p. 7) in order to obtain the wisdom you need to make strength-based decisions. The reality of any situation and the clear, unencumbered thinking of the situation helps our mind and brain make sense of the past and the present. In fact, by transforming the emotional information that goes along with challenging experiences, we have the potential to change our brain and avoid the trap of automatic conclusions. Mindful awareness of why we respond or think as we do will allow us to accept our experiences as a learning ground. It allows us to reflect and learn from each experience. Embrace each of your emotional experiences and the information you glean from them, and then trade them in for life-changing awareness. Life-changing awareness and self-knowledge is the child of experiential wisdom.

You can determine hidden motives and intentions that drive human behaviors and abilities through experiential wisdom buildup. Experiential wisdom involves having the confidence and courage to dredge up wisdom from emotional experiences. Experiential wisdom is one remedy that will help free you from any obsessive preoccupations with negative emotions and negative thinking patterns that lead to anger, anxiety, and depression. Experiential wisdom allows us to reappraise the validity of an emotion and to correctly look at in the context of a situation. If you become emotionally stirred up for any reason, it behooves you to ask yourself why, and then re-evaluate the reason for your reaction.

With the absence of emotional involvement, your mind will allow you to focus on the present and participate in self-examination. Once you have built up a strong trust in the power of experiential wisdom, you will have a better sense of the hidden motives and intentions of others and yourself.

This development of a second sense will allow you to regulate how you should behave.

Since the path to experiential wisdom involves the recognition of thought, intent and behavior, it's ensuing affect on your life will result in stronger decision-making. To many it may seem that wisdom is gained by years of living and experience. However, we all know people for whom age did not result in wisdom of any kind. Simply put, gathering all the personal resources you have on hand—those mentioned in this book—and collectively paying attention to them, you can't help but make wise decisions. Being able to easily make wise decisions that directly impact your existence, your actions, and your wellbeing, will temper and enhance the quality of all your interactions.

Relationships and Wisdom

The same principle of listening to your spirit that is involved in making wise decisions also relates to choosing a mate. It often seems that while we are busy making important choices in our lives, the choosing of a mate is left to arbitrary reasoning like, "He's cute." The haunting reality is that we often choose a mate that not only doesn't fulfill our expectations of a relationship, but turns out to be a repeat of past failed relationships.

On the one hand, many of us behave as though anyone will make a good mate so long as we perceive he or she loves us. On the other hand, there are others who tackle the search for a mate with a shopping list without a mention of character, integrity, loyalty and other important qualities necessary for a successful relationship.

They may a sense of humor, a sense of adventure, someone who owns their own business, likes to travel, and work out. The fact of the matter is, that in spite of our list, or the lack thereof, people often attract individuals with few, if any, of the qualities important for a good match.

The question then becomes why? Where is the wisdom in that? Wisdom dictates that we look at the reality of a person's character and their behaviors, noting seriously the red flags that always present themselves at the beginning of any relationship. Red flags are reality and should never be discounted or marginalized. Maya Angelou was succinct in noting the truth of the situation when she said, "When someone tells you who they are, believe them the first time." In short, wisdom considers the reality of everything—whether you like it or not.

It is often said that we teach people how to treat us. What we tolerate and overlook will determine the kind of treatment we get in any relationship regardless of what we want or say we want. Decide now how you want to be treated and correct it if you must, but correct the behavior immediately. The wise thing is to pay attention to the kind of person you are when you are with a particular person. Does that person elevate who you are or make you a better person for knowing them? Do they contribute to the overall wellbeing of your life? Do they value who you are in an unconditional manner? The ability to appreciate the complete truth of a person and to act on that in every situation is wisdom. Ignite your ability to be wise. "Experiential wisdom is spiritual wealth" –Les Brown'

The wisdom of non-negotiable principles

Non-negotiable principles are an important foundation for making decisions that are both strong (strength-based) and support your life. Non-negotiable principles have the power to guarantee a successful outcome of most decisions. It is the foundation for making decisions that feed your life's goals. It is your balance, a means to an end, and an equalizer to fate. Deciding to apply non-negotiable principles to your choices is the sensible person's solution to haste, waste, and indecision. Non-negotiable principles require that you keep reign on any emotions that may lead you astray, but non-negotiable principles are also where your perseverance can be found.

The faithful honoring of your principles will stop foolishness, unleash clarity, and keep you on track for what you want in your life. Non-negotiable principles do much for steadying your life. They are viable coping mechanisms for when you unexpectedly meet with disappointment, opposition, or complicated decisions. You can always rest on your principles to keep your life in a contented state. It doesn't mean that your life will be free of problems or disasters, but your principles will keep you on track for what you want out of your life and the lives of your loved ones.

The variable of influence, past experiences, growth and maturity will potentially grow the nature of your non-negotiable principles, and reflect who you are and what you want out of life. Non-negotiable principles, by definition, are values about which you do not compromise or negotiate to change even a little bit. Abandoning your principles is never an option. Non-negotiable means unchangeable. Your non-negotiable principles are your core values—standards that you have decided make up the basis of how you intend to live your life. Above everything, your non-negotiables establish boundaries no one should ever be allowed to cross. Boundaries and non-negotiables ensure that you are respected—you, your opinions, your choices, and your ideals. Non-Negotiable principles make a difference in your life and ultimately in the lives of those close to you.

Establishing your own non-negotiable principles begin with defining what principles you will steadfastly live by. They are principles vital to you—not anyone else. It establishes who you are to others and is the basis for creating healthy relationships, a contented wellbeing, and an uncompromising life. It is one of the things that are the backbone for acquiring inward strength and determination. It will allow you to acquire the strength to boldly be who you are and doggedly maintain respect for yourself.

Setting and sustaining boundaries is a skill. Unfortunately, it's a skill many of us fail to learn. It may be true that you've picked up ideas from past experiences or by watching others who have demonstrated their own non-negotiable principles, but you must establish your own.

Non-negotiable principles help you build healthy boundaries. Healthy boundaries mean knowing and understanding what your limits are. It means respecting who you are and refusing to lose yourself.

An example of a loss of self is Margaret. Margaret was married to Jason for almost ten years. In the 10th month of the 10th year, they divorced. Margaret's first response was relief. She finally felt she could live her life just as she wanted. She was concerned that at age forty she would never live the life she had intended. She had subjugated all her wants in favor of what Jason wanted and said he needed. For almost ten years, the real Margaret never surfaced.

The day after the divorce was final, Margaret headed for the grocery store. Her goal was to finally buy the foods she liked and wanted to eat. She walked around the grocery store picking up one thing then another, and then replacing them on the shelf. She did this for more than an hour and in the end, she left the store empty handed. She was choosing foods she thought she liked when she realized all her choices were Jason's favorites, not her choices at all. She was so unaccustomed to listening to what she wanted and what she liked that she had no idea what kind of food she liked.

Margaret surrendered all she was in favor of supporting Jason's life. A full and satisfying relationship never requires a loss of self, a loss of personal ideals, or a loss of personal growth. It didn't take much of a nudge to convince Margaret to think about who she really is and to establish non-negotiable principles to make sure others would always respect who she is.

Take time to analyze who you are, what you like, what you don't like, and most importantly, how you want the significant people in your life to treat you. Boundaries and non-negotiable principles are all about honing in on your feelings and then being sure to honor them.

If you notice yourself slipping or failing to maintain a boundary, ask yourself why and what has changed. Take notice of what you or the other person in any situation is doing. Take notice of what about any situation makes you stressed or resentful. Then, mull over your options. Decide what you will do about the situation. Don't worry about how long it may take for you to have a response—just respond. You will get better at expressing yourself in time.

Essential to establishing non-negotiable principles—like it is for establishing a boundary—is to become aware of who you really are and what you really want out of life. Look into the rules you have already established and ask yourself whether or not those rules serve you. Ask yourself whether they are compatible with the you inside. Take time to become aware of you—what you want, what elevates your character and wellbeing, what you need, and what makes you content.

Awareness of self carries with it tremendous power. To take advantage of that power, you have to differentiate between boundaries that are crossable and those that are not. Crossable boundaries are those you would like to be met, but are not deal-breakers. If they are violated, it won't be life shattering to the fundamental essence of who you are. However, if you become upset, it is possible that a non-negotiable principle has been violated. You must create a set of rules that are serious deal-breakers—a non-negotiable. Rules you should never tolerate being violated because these violations are an attack on your fundamental essence, your soul, and what you stand for. Awareness of yourself gives you choice. It allows you to make decisions that enlarge your world, participate in your growth, and support your ability to be truly happy.

The powerful thing about being intimately acquainted with yourself is that you establish the foundation for living a life that is truly of your own design. It allows you to establish rules that support your aims and your existence. When you assert your power of choice—make strength-based decisions—you gain control and self-confidence over the one life you have on this earth.

You can determine when a non-negotiable principle is being violated when you find yourself in an uncomfortable situation. Ask yourself what are the feelings you are feeling and what exactly causes you to have those feelings? Ask yourself what is it about a particular interaction or a person's expectation that bothers you?

A common feeling that occurs when a non-negotiable principle has been violated is a slight feeling of resentment. Resentment usually comes from being taken advantage of or not being appreciated. It is often a sign that you are pushing yourself beyond your own boundary. For example, when you begin to feel guilty, you are probably about to give up a boundary in favor of someone else's wishes or requirements. Abandoning one of your non-negotiable principles because someone thinks as they think you should may bring on a feeling of resentment. Your feeling of resentment is simply a signal that you are abandoning a non-negotiable principle and your soul is rebelling.

Someone else has imposed his or her expectations, views, values or behavior criteria, on you and you are allowing it. Remember, non-negotiable principles are non-negotiable. You must respect yourself and your life, and not give in to fear or a lack of courage. Insist they not cross your boundary. This is your life and you get only one chance at it. It is quite possible that the person for whom you are abandoning your principle has principles of their own and would never consider abandoning them for you.

Be aware that boundary setting is a two-way street and requires more than just creating rules. A problem may occur if you fail to tell others about your boundaries or fail to consistently insist on them. A failure to insist on a boundary can have a number of reasons that lack valid motives. For example, you may not want to hurt someone's feelings, or think your boundary or non-negotiable is not that important. You may incorrectly reason that it doesn't matter if you just keep doing what others want regardless of your own wishes. You may think that compliance eliminates conflict and promotes an easy life, but you would be wrong. You may fear making a person upset, angry, or insulted, but they'll get over it.

There are no excuses or reasons for not defending your boundaries; they are simply the result of fear. (Review the section on The Fear of Criticism.) Too often, women neglect to stand up for themselves in order to avoid confrontation. To rightly analyze a boundary violation ask your self, "How much of the situation is really about me? How much of it is really about the other person? What do I need to do (if anything) to regain my personal power and stand up for myself?

Give yourself permission to have non-negotiables and enforce them. Fear, guilt and self-doubt are pitfalls. You may wonder if you even deserve to have a non-negotiable. Everyone deserves to maintain self. Ignore any fear you may have of a person's response to your request to adhere to a boundary.

Boundaries aren't just a sign of a healthy relationship; they are a sign of your self-respect. Give yourself permission to set boundaries and don't be embarrassed to preserve them.

Sometimes setting boundaries is hard work, and takes time and effort. But most importantly, it takes consistency. You have to stick with your values and ideals. How you relate to people, and how they relate to you, is a result of the boundaries you enforce.

Learn to set boundaries with everyone and have the courage to enforce your non-negotiables with everyone; even those who tend to intimidate you. Find the words you need to say when someone is intent on violating one of your non-negotiables. You can't be a truly contented person if others disrespect you or ignore the boundaries you deem important. So, don't feel guilty about having boundaries.

Get rid of any obstacles that block your way to enforcing a boundary. Remember, boundaries and non-negotiables determine and maintain who you are. You can't set strong non-negotiables if you are unsure of where you stand. Identify your physical, emotional, mental and spiritual limits. Consider what you can tolerate and accept, and decide what makes you feel uncomfortable or stressed. It is your feelings that will help you identify what your limits are and what boundaries and non-negotiables you must establish. So, tune into your feelings and construct your non-negotiable list.

There are two key feelings of which to be aware—discomfort and resentment. They are red flags that indicate you are allowing one of your non-negotiables to be violated. When someone acts in a way that makes you feel uncomfortable, it is a cue that they may be ignoring one of your non-negotiables.

Once you realize what may be going on, be direct. Your words don't have to be elaborate or semantically correct. It is okay to stumble over your words, show nervousness, or be uneasy. It is only important that you be direct and reveal what you want without apology. Say whatever you need to say, in whatever way you are able to say it. You will get better at expressing your desires and making your wants known over time. More importantly however, you will feel better and you will live a more spiritually comfortable life when people respect who you are.

Obstacles to Non-negotiables

Consider your past and present. Your history may be an obstacle to correctly identifying non-negotiable violations. Consider how you were raised along with your role in your family. If you held the role of caretaker, you learned to focus on others and allowing yourself to be drained emotionally or physically. Ignoring your own needs might have become the norm for you.

Think about the people with whom you surround yourself. Are your relationships reciprocal? Do they allow a healthy give and take? Do they allow for you to have a non-negotiable? Is respect a central core of the relationship?

Consider that your environment may be unhealthy as well. You may question your non-negotiable enforcement if you are the only one standing for a principle or if you don't conform to what everyone else is doing.

Give yourself permission to put yourself first. No, it is not selfish. We all know the difference between being selfish and when it is necessary to consider yourself first. Remember, you count too. So does your physical and mental health.

Self-care also means recognizing the importance of your feelings and honoring them. Your feelings serve as important cues about your wellbeing and about what makes you happy or unhappy. When you put yourself first, you will find you have the energy, peace of mind, and positive outlook to be more present with others. You in turn will more available for them. When you are in a better place, you can be a better wife, mother, husband, co-worker or friend.

Establishing Non-negotiables

If you're having a hard time establishing non-negotiables, get support from like-minded individuals. Seek the help of a therapist, a support group, or a good friend.

It is not enough to just create a non-negotiable. You will have to let others know what those non-negotiables are. In other words, you will have to become comfortable with being straightforward and honest. Don't expect others to guess or figure out what you want or need because they won't. Whenever a situation presents itself, you will have to communicate your discomfort or distress at the time it happens. When you do, you make sure others become familiar with your boundaries. Make sure they know what you expect and what you want. You will have to gather the courage God has already instilled in you and use the strength you instinctively know you can muster to let people know when they have crossed a line that is not acceptable to you.

Creating Your Non-negotiables

Communicating your non-negotiable principles doesn't mean you have to deliver the information with anger or irritation. A simple statement of fact in a neutral tone is enough; "I don't like what you are doing," or "I don't allow that," or "I don't want you to speak to me that way."

You can be firm and still be graceful. There is no need to defend, argue, or explain your feelings. State what you have to say and stay strong. If you give in or back down, you invite people to ignore your needs. You invite disrespect, neglect, mistreatment, and inattention.

Here are examples of situations that may require you to communicate a boundary or non-negotiable. It is important that when and if you are faced with similar situations that you respond in a way that will enforce what you need.

Examples are when:

- You have to confront an angry person: "If you continue to yell at me, I'll have to ask you to leave."
- Someone is critical of you: "It's not okay for you talk badly about my work to others. I don't allow people to disrespect me in that manner."
- A relative borrows money far too often or takes advantage of your generosity: "I am not going to lend you anymore money. I love you, but I am not responsible for your lifestyle. You are responsible for your life."

PILLAR REFLECTION SECTION: WISDOM

List the fears that resulted in foolishness?

_____

_____

_____

_____

_____

_____

_____

_____

_____

_____

_____

_____

_____

_____

Pillar Action Section: Wisdom

What are the lessons or blessings you've learned to use in your life?

_____

_____

_____

_____

_____

_____

_____

_____

_____

_____

_____

_____

Please bring your questions about this pillar to Decision Time live event or a complimentary call with Stone Love.

NOTES

PILLAR THREE: INTUITION

To exercise your ability to make decisions with strength and confidence, you must also listen to what your intuition is saying. Intuition is the ability to understand something immediately without the need for conscious reasoning. It is the power to know something without the benefit of being able to explain it rationally. Our culture has drummed into us that rational thought must always rule. We have been taught that following our intuitive instruction is foolish and should never be obeyed. However, we have also learned that our rational evaluations aren't always correct. Someone once said, "I seem to make my worse decisions when I am doing my best rational thinking." What this has caused us to do is to question the certainty of solely relying on ration thought. Instead, we are prompted to ask, what about that "inner voice," that gut feeling and un-named little something that comes from within telling us there is something beneath our layers of logic. When making a decision, large or small, insignificant or important, your intuition is looking to guide you. Give credit to what the 'god' in you is trying to tell you and whatever you do, don't ignore the message.

Intuition, as important as it is, is not the same as instinct. The words intuition and instinct are often used inter-changeably but they are completely different. Intuition is an innate knowledge or belief of something you can't explain but you know is right. Instinct on the other hand, is an autonomic response to stimuli without thought. For example a duck instinctively knows when to leave one climate for another. He instinctive knows when to mate, how far to fly, and when to seek safety. Ducks do these things without reasoning. Ducks do not know why. They merely obey the instincts God placed within them. An instinctive action for a human is to raise your hand when it appears someone might strike you. Instinct is a natural behavior that functions according to fixed patterns, but intuition is a mental process that happens outside the realm of preset behaviors.

Intuition is a process that takes place in the mind. It uses past events, and insignificant information and unrecognized trivia to aid our perception. With intuition, you may find that somehow you are able to perceive things and situations that are not plainly evident. It is an unexplainable insight that nudges you to see beyond the obvious. For example, you may sense that someone is not telling you the truth. You have no explanation for it, but your gut tells you something is not right. Intuition is the thoughts and feelings you have about a particular matter that cannot be explained or justified by logic, and are often correct.

Your spirit is disseminating emotions, experiences, feelings, and acquired knowledge that result in giving you what is called intuitive instruction. It is intuition that is prompting you— instructing you—to consider what you are feeling and what your other faculties are saying. Our mind has the ability to archive all kinds of information not logged in on a conscious level. We often pick up information subconsciously without comprehending it, such as body language, tone of voice, or a particular look. Remember, intuitive instruction is one of the strong pillars on which strength-based decisions are made possible.

Malcolm Gladwell, in his book *Blink: The Power of Thinking Without Thinking,* takes a long hard look at the inner workings of human intuition. He presents theories that suggest our mental processes work quickly and automatically with relatively little information. He provides evidence that expert judgment and instantaneous decisions are often right without the need of extensive knowledge. He looks into the drawbacks that prevent us from using our intuition and the influences that destroy the mechanisms of intuition.

Intuition has the ability to talk to us in unexpected ways. It works with both your conscious and your unconscious. It also uses your body to send messages unique to you. Physical reactions are a signal that your intuition is working. You've may have heard it said that, "He makes the hairs on the back of my neck stand up." That is intuition using your body to signal something is wrong. It may be telling you that in some way, the person in question is unsafe. You may experience a tingle, a feeling in your stomach, or an unsettling emotion of some kind. It may be your intuition sending you a message in an attempt to protect you.

It is quite possible that your intuition has been working for you your entire life and has always sent you messages that should have been heeded. So, pay attention to your intuition and watch for any physical responses that may be intuition sending you a message.

Decisions are never arbitrary choices; they are made—good or bad—as the result of the various internal and external forces we have talked about in this book so far. In matters of decisions, your intuitive instructor is another one of those forces that contribute to your strengths. Your intuitive instructor is your spirit acting as your guardian. When attempting to listen to your spirit even when it appears to ignore logic, enlist your unfiltered courage. Be mindful that it is essential to take care when listening to your intuition. Make sure you learn how to recognize when it is intuition is speaking to you.

The voice of intuition can be so strong and so persistent that it leaves you without rest until you carry out its dictates. You can learn to fully recognize your intuition's nudging in time and with practice. And when you do, a feeling of persistent or nudging should always get your attention.

Lucinda is an example of how the power of intuition played a part in her life. A strong and powerful nudging came to Lucinda one fall evening while on a church retreat. It was raining and storming when she arrived late to the retreat's remote mountain location. The minute she stepped up to the reception table to register she had a disturbing feeling she should head home immediately. Instead of leaving however, Lucinda's rational thought process kicked in, "It's late, I'm tired, and besides, it's dangerous to drive in a storm." She dismissed her feelings and registered. Later, while in her room, another strong prodding warned her. To appease the feeling, she told herself she would leave first thing in the morning. "The rain would have subsided by then," she told herself.

That night Lucinda didn't sleep well. She had disturbing dreams she had difficulty recalling. Upon waking the next morning, Lucinda discovered an unforeseen storm had covered everything in snow and ice. She was trapped. Messages from retreat organizers instructed everyone to leave immediately. The storm was going to get worse. Lucinda jumped in her car but on the way down the mountain, it careened out of control and almost flung her over the mountainside. It was only by chance that a tow truck was minutes behind her. They witnessed the accident and were able to pull her to safety without further incidence. If the tow truck had not been there, Lucinda might not have survived the slick icy roadway. There would have been no question of safety if Lucinda had heeded her intuition and left as instructed.

Lucinda's nature was one that relied solely on rational thought. There was however something to be said for her inner voice, that something she couldn't name that worked to alert and warn her. Watch for your intuitive instructor. Pay attention to it. Get to know it. No, it isn't the only thing that works with our spirit, but it is one of many important things. Trust your instincts. It can be difficult to depend on something you don't understand, and you should not base everything on intuition alone, but, if you have weighed all your options and the answer still does not present itself, it may be time to enlist your intuition. Throw caution to the wind and listen, and you will begin to release the real you.

PILLAR REFLECTION SECTION: INTUITION

Think back to the moment you Intuitively knew better. What flawed reasoning or logic did you use to talk you out of your good sense?

_____

_____

_____

_____

_____

_____

_____

_____

_____

_____

_____

_____

PILLAR ACTION SECTION: INTUITION What would have been your results if you would have listened to your intuition?

_____

_____

_____

_____

_____

_____

_____

_____

_____

_____

_____

_____

_____

Please bring your questions about this pillar to Decision Time live event or a complimentary call with Stone Love.

NOTES

NOTES

PILLAR FOUR: INITIATIVE

When making a strength-based decision, test the validity of your choices by asking yourself, if any of your decisions originate with you. Did you initiate the choice you are making or want to make? Is your choice the prompting of others? Are you accepting someone else's agenda? Or are you merely conforming to the wishes and directives of someone else's, beliefs, expectations, and/or standards? Ask yourself, "Am I truly making this decision of my own volition and for the benefit of the life I want to lead?"

Individuals who initiate their own course of action are asserting their choices and using their own volition. Demonstrating your own initiative is a required step to making decisions that reflect your true wants and desires. It is a requirement of strength-based decision making. It is another one of those actions you must take to be sure you are taking your life down the exact road you want to travel. There are many historical accounts of phenomenal successes that were the result of decisions initiated by individuals who stood alone, but who knew what they wanted and where they wanted to go. Their decisions weren't always popular or respected, but they were instigated by people unafraid to take the initiative.

Personal initiative means taking yourself to task. It means taking your life in your own hands and being the sole driver of it. It means that you can't wait for someone else to suggest a course of action or approve. You have to analyze the situation for yourself and come up with ideas and plans of your own. Yes, it is a big step, but an essential step. Only you know what you need.

Practically everything we do on this earth is born out of initiative. Initiative is the act of starting something and evaluating it with fresh eyes. It is a new way to think about old problems. It means forging ahead on an old path in a different direction without anyone telling you to do so.

Personal initiative is the ability to create, nurture and give life to a spirit-driven plan with the abilities and creativity you already have at your disposal. Like all the pillars before this one, you cannot be afraid to initiate a new behavior or be afraid to embark on a new life without the approval or go-ahead of someone else. You have a God-given mandate to be a person of vision and new ideas. Get comfortable with the idea of creating things anew and leading a different kind of life. Do this right now by taking the initiative to put it into action. Later we will talk about the importance of finishing what you start, but for now, get started and move without fear, hesitation, or anticipated regret. Take the initiative to make change fervently and with passion.

Know this, there will always be things you need in order to follow through on your objective once you initiate it. You may need money, a new skill, time, technical know-how, education, etc. But, you can tackle those things later. For now, fearlessly begin your change and do it with purpose. The uniqueness of your personality and the determination you will acquire by making strength-based decisions will allow you to achieve new and better results—results unique to you.

PILLAR REFLECTION SECTION: INITIATIVE

The opposite of using your personal initiative is allowing someone else to cower and douse the fire in your belly with his or her own initiative. Why did you allow that?

_____

_____

_____

_____

_____

_____

_____

_____

_____

_____

_____

_____

_____

_____

Pillar Action Section: initiative

What new habits or practices will you adopt going forward? How will you fuel your new habits and practices going forward?

_____

_____

_____

_____

_____

_____

_____

_____

_____

_____

_____

_____

_____

Please bring your questions about this pillar to Decision Time live event or a complimentary call with Stone Love.

_____

_____

_____

_____

_____

_____

_____

_____

_____

_____

_____

_____

_____

_____

NOTES

PILLAR FIVE: WILLINGNESS

The next question in the list of things necessary for making strength-based decision is to ask yourself, "Do you have a willing spirit?"

So far, you have measured the intensity of your strength-based decisions by considering whether the decision sits well with your spirit and whether you have an inward peace about it. Then, you measured your options through the reliable eyes of wisdom asking if is it a wise choice for you. Next, you looked at the power intuition plays in the your choices. You looked at what your inner voice has to say and you listened. And consequently, you analyzed whether you were initiating the actions you intended for yourself and noted whether your decisions were someone else's idea.

When you aim at making a decision, you have to take into consideration that intention or desire is not enough. You have to acknowledge the difference between wanting to do something and the eventual reality of actually having to do it.

Follow-through is the next important order of business. It may be that your spirit is willing, but you have neither the ability nor the inclination to act on a particular decision. You also have to decide whether you are willing to take on the responsibility for the decisions you are about make. You have to be willing to deal with the results of your decision before you make the decision, because if your decisions are going to have the strength of your convictions and a loyalty to self, you have to acknowledge the probable resulting circumstances.

Take the necessary time you need to recognize the role you may have to play in your final decisions and then assess your willingness to follow through. Tell the truth. Be honest to yourself and to others by acknowledging that the responsibility is yours and that you will stand by your decision. The key to success is not to make decisions you aren't prepared to manage or cope with later. You can choose to be a helpless victim of your own habits and poor decisions, or you can make strength-based decisions according to the steps laid out in this book. You can choose to live your life as you always have or you can choose the alternative that gives you the life you want.

We all know there is a difference between needing to do something and the willingness to do something. You may need to stop smoking or drinking, but if you are unwilling to do what it takes to stop you will never make progress. When you assume the responsibility of a particular course of action and analyze with honesty whether you are actually willing to commit to the decision, then you will do it without sabotaging yourself or repeatedly hiding behind false excuses.

You have the God-given freedom of will and the power to control your own thoughts. You have control of every deliberate action you take. You can choose your behaviors. You can decide if you will be strong-willed or weak-willed. You can decide your purpose and you can act accordingly. When you make those decisions, you will be making strength-based decisions.

PILLAR REFLECTION SECTION: WILLINGNESS

Denial and reluctance causes resistance. If you didn't resist it, then what would be the effect?

_____

_____

_____

_____

_____

_____

_____

_____

_____

_____

_____

_____

Pillar Action Section: Willingness

Learn not to resist. Trust and allow the process to build up
your willing spirit. How will you do that?

_____

_____

_____

_____

_____

_____

_____

_____

_____

_____

Please bring your questions about this pillar to Decision Time live event or a complimentary call with Stone Love.

_____

_____

_____

_____

_____

_____

_____

_____

_____

_____

_____

_____

_____

NOTES

PILLAR SIX: THE QUINT-ESSENTIALS

Consider the four human aspects that affect decisions. They are spiritual, mental, physical, financial and temporal (time). You must take into consideration all these qualities play in your resolve to make strength-based decisions. You can't be mentally ready to change your life and fail to be spiritually ready. You can't be emotionally ready and not financially ready. You can't be physically vigorous and not financially invested. All the quint-essentials and every pillar are the foundations upon which personal strengths and a life of personal determination are built.

Emotional:

When making a strength-based decision, being invested with mental clarity is essential. The lack of focus can draw a compromised conclusion. With clarity of mind, straightforwardness of purpose, we can detect false data that leads to faulty deduction and reasoning. Distractions, both large and small, affect your ability to think clearly. Most of us have been haunted by decisions we've made under duress—decisions made with a mind compromised by time constraints, insignificant events, and other distractions—mind compromising decisions. A sound mind recognizes and isolates any biases or distractions that may weaken one's mental state. Your mental wellbeing is an important matter when making a decision. Decisions made in haste and without consideration to one's own mental state can leave mental scars and rob you of your ability to trust your own capabilities and innate talents.

Paying attention to the mental constraints affect decisions is a skill. Caring for and building up your mental resources will allow you to thrive and enjoy longevity. Seek out mental exercises that will nourish your brain and keep you prepared to make strength-based decisions. Your mental foundations are such an important factor to clear thinking and clear judgment that you should never engage in decision making unless you are able to be clear minded and free of biases.

Physical:

Your health and physical wellness contributes to you mental clarity. Your physical state always affects our decisions. If we are sick, it is likely we will make an ill-fated decision based solely on how we are feeling. Pain and discomfort block both clear and analytical decision capabilities. Do nothing; decide nothing if you do not feel well. Take care of your body so it can take care of your mind.

Financial:

Pride of ownership, and the peace and confidence that comes from having enough money is the crux of this essential. Too often our ability to make progress towards our passions are limited by a lack of money. We put the burden of the 'here and now' first on our to-do lists: job security, mortgage, credit cards, automobile concerns, health insurance, and on and on. But the important passions in our lives go to the end of list—if they actually make it on the list at all. Our dreams and passions are most often relegated to a space when we think we will have more time—which we never seem to have. Financial stability is a quint-essential that makes it possible to work on dreams without worry or conflict. We are not talking about being wealthy. We are talking about having enough money so that you can live without the worry and stress that comes with lack.

Financial stability gives you the freedom to live and work on your own terms. It eliminates tension and promotes the belief in positive outcomes. Being financially stable means that you have to be financially responsibility and make the handling of what money you do have an important part of your strength-based plan. Spend wisely, save, and make responsible financial decisions.

Spiritual:

The spirit is a presence only you can define. Some say it is divine. We must be keenly aware of the power of spirit to lead us through the material world especially when it comes to making a decision. Our spiritual presence is a whisper you can't hear, but can feel. Your spiritual presence can tell a story about you before you can think of your own. It precedes you. This is why, in its purest form, your spirit can be more potent than the voice of a thousand individuals. If you follow spirit's instructions and warnings, and trust in spirit's perception, it will guide you into making each decision a strength-based decision. Think of your spirit as an entity with a mind of its own. Consult with it. Allow it to speak to you as only your best self could. If you listen, you will add another dimension to your good intentions, your goals, and your life. A strong spirit can overcome difficulties, change circumstances for the better, and lift you to heights you didn't think you could reach. A determined spirit wins gold metals, ensures survival in a snowstorm, and creates success out of failure.

Temporal (Time):

The chief quint-essential is the most important. It is time. We can't create more time, but we can do more in the time allotted. And regardless of whether we like it or not, there is an appointed time for everything. We cannot force things and we cannot delay them. As people are often fond of saying, "nothing happens before its time." There is a life and death freedom about recognizing the power and constraints of time. Dr. Soren, a character in the movie *Star Trek: Generations,* is anxious to live forever with his family in the vortex. In the movie he says, "Time is the fire in which we burn." In other words, time controls us and it demands respect.

Time is the one universal, non-negotiable agreement we are forced to make with life. No decision can be made without considering time. Time will not allow a lie to live forever, because eventually, the truth will come out. Time will not allow justice to go unheeded. It will not allow its squander to go unpunished. You must consider time in all things. A conscious recognition of time will help you make life-changing decisions accurately and when they will serve you best.

PILLAR REFLECTION SECTION: THE QUINT-ESSENTIALS

Grasping all five of the Quint-Essentials will allow you the power to pack a powerful punch. Knowing this, how will you get exactly what you want?

_____

_____

_____

_____

_____

_____

_____

_____

_____

_____

_____

_____

Pillar Action Section: The Quint-Essentials

Beyond the Quint-Essentials carefully review your options and use moderation when making a strength-based decision.

_____

_____

_____

_____

_____

_____

_____

_____

_____

_____

_____

_____

Please bring your questions about this pillar to Decision Time live event or a complimentary call with Stone Love.

NOTES

PILLAR SEVEN: THE DISCERNMENT TRIAD

Discernment is having an innate insight about the realities of any situation in the here and now. It is the ability to perceive what is true, right, and lasting. Discernment is simultaneously using all the information you've gleaned throughout your life and using it to make conclusions about your current situation. It is using all the information in this book to make both an empowering decision and a decision right for you.

It is often thought that discernment is a talent impossible to teach. However, you can acquire the skill of discernment by paying close attention to the essential triad of discernment skills: identifying emotional triggers, recognizing reality, and judging the spirit in which a happening is perceived.

Triggers

A trigger is something that forces an emotional response without thought or planning. Triggers are automatic responses you did not initiate and may have not chosen. Triggered responses are the adversary to your wishes and intentions. They force you to lie about our purpose and intent. They act so quickly that they have the power to make liars of us all. Instead of paying attention to exactly why your response is so dramatic, you rationalize it to make sense to your brain. You lie to yourself and to others who witness a triggered response.

Triggers can block your ability to determine what is happening in any given situation. It can obstruct your sensibilities for recognizing truth, honesty, and reality. It also has the power to cause you to overlook signs pointing you in the right direction.

Triggered emotions are nothing more than survival mechanisms. They are emotions that come from making lose associations to events that may or may not have anything to do with the reality at the moment. Triggered responses do not serve you for the better. They often result in the loss of important relationship or important opportunities.

You are ultimately responsible recognizing trigger situations, stopping them and making an effort to change those unconscious reactions. It may take some investigative work on your part, but you must determine where an emotion lives and then challenge it. Ask yourself if you are responding to a feeling of hurt or the reliving a past injustice. Ask yourself if you are reacting to an irrational fear, a fear of commitment, a fear of the unknown, or a fear of criticism. The key to stopping any trigger from manifesting itself is to recognize each and every time you react without intention.

To prevent triggers from ruining your life:
- Don't judge your emotional response when triggered by an event.
- Don't say anything to yourself that you wouldn't say to the face of someone you care about or not.
- Do not rationalize your behavior; rationalization and justification will not put you back in control of your responses. Rationalizing will not allow false feelings to dissipate.
- Dive deeper into a situation to determine exactly what the issue is. Keep a journal and write down your responses if you have to, but search a trigger's origins.
- Investigate when an issue may have first occurred and analyze it until it makes sense or becomes clear.
- Breathe. Breathing is a great diffuser to any emotional upset. Center yourself. Sit and take a short break. Breathe deeply. Use whatever gestures may help you relax.
- Stay in the here and now so you can name the emotion you are feeling. Are you angry, hurt, disappointed or rejected?

- All in all, learn to be patient with yourself. Search for the precise event that is triggering a response or mood. It's a subtle talent that takes practice. Learn what environments, situations, or events trigger an autonomic response, and then figure out why. It is this figuring that will allow you to stop being manipulated by situations.

Recognition of Reality

Whatever circumstance you may be in, you need to acknowledge the fact that you exist in the here and now. Survival requires us to see things as they really are and not to dwell on how we wish things to be. Ignoring reality drains you of your physical, and emotional reserves and contaminates your thought processes.

We have already talked about the danger of participating in poor thinking habits earlier in this book. So, instead of false optimism about your possibilities and your future, refuse to ignore reality. Ignoring reality may make you prone to negative thinking, and the doubts and fears that can come with negative thinking.

A failure to accept may allow your subconscious to have you take on the role of victim. A failure to acknowledge and appreciate the reality of any situation ends in the creation of false excuses as to why things are not as you expected them to be. Everyone benefits when you recognize and acknowledge the full reality of what actually is. Embrace the idea that accepting reality may mean leaving your comfort zone, and accepting loss and rejection. Choosing to see reality requires courage and determination. You will have those qualities in abundance when you decide to live in the here and now. False realities are just that, false.

Judging intention and the spirit in which it is given.

Stephen Covey said it is important to "Judge ourselves by our intentions and others by their behavior" and Peter Drucker said, "The most important thing in communication is hearing what isn't said." The silent signals of nonverbal communication tend to reveal hidden motives and emotions. They can reveal in others a feeling of fear, honesty, joy, indecision, frustration, and much more. The smallest gesture, like the way a stranger stands or enters a room, can speak volumes about their self-confidence. It is readily believed by most that a person can hide their intentions or emotions. But there is a silent language that gives them away. Our bodies often—without our wanting them to—disclose just what our intentions are. The goal to becoming discerning means that you will have to watch for those signals and pay attention to what those signals are saying. It is a scientific reality that gestures give away our true intentions, and try as we may, tell the tale anyway. Body language knowledge is a tool essential for discerning people, situations, and making strength-based decisions. It behooves you to learn how to interpret non-verbal language, as well as the gestures and actions that reveal thoughts, attitudes, and emotions. Children have little trouble ascertaining the meaning of body language because they experience the world through intuition. They watch for reactions and test behaviors. And they are seldom wrong.

Whatever knowledge you use to judge others, pay special attention to body language because it will allow you to deal effectively with people, protect yourself, and help those who may need your help.

Below are a few last thoughts to add to the points we have made in this book. These last points are designed to make your journey to achievement, accomplishment, and brilliance even more attainable.

1. **Be sure to take action on every decision immediately.**

Take inspired action. Put the pillars into action to master them. Time is always of the essence. If you practice the 7 pillars for making strength-based decisions, you have done your due diligence to making your life your own. Once you are confident that you have made your decision with strength, move on your decision immediately. Don't procrastinate; time waits for no one. Practice the pillars of the decision-making process so you can master then and call on their skills when needed.

2. **Your life is your own. Take your control back.**

To focus on where you have lost your control or allowed it to be taken, begin to list all the things you have always wanted to do but have not done. Now, list those things—perceived or real—that have kept you from doing those things. Once you have listed everything you can think of, take a good hard look at whether those things truly kept you from obtaining your goal. If you honestly evaluate your list, the chances are that the biggest obstacle was you. There a few instances where adults aren't able to accomplish what they want if they are determined, creative, and believe strongly in themselves.

"There is no chance, no destiny, no fate, that can hinder the firm resolve of a determined soul." -Ella Wheeler Wilcox.

If you are unsure of this fact, perhaps the poem Invictus, by William Ernest Henley, may convince you:

Invictus

Out of the night that covers me,
Black as the pit from pole to pole,
I thank whatever gods may be
For my unconquerable soul.
In the fell clutch of circumstance
I have not winced nor cried aloud.
Under the bludgeonings of chance
My head is bloody, but unbowed.
Beyond this place of wrath and tears
Looms but the Horror of the shade,
And yet the menace of the years
Finds and shall find me unafraid.
It matters not how strait the gate,
How charged with punishments the scroll,
I am the master of my fate,
I am the captain of my soul.

Now, write down all the ways you can go about changing each obstacle into a green light for doing the things you want to do and becoming the kind of person you want to be. As you work with your list, remind yourself that you are a unique individual with talents and abilities all your own. Important people may have said otherwise, but they were wrong. God never leaves us without a way up and out. If you have trouble believing this fact, look at Stephen Hawkings, the scientific genius who is unable to move or talk but makes incredible discoveries about our universe.

You have the ability to resolve problems and work on how to resolve them. It is more than possible for you to do away with your obstacles. You can do it slowly or quickly. You can take small steps or big ones. It is all up to you. Your future is entirely in your hands. You are in control of your life whether you believe it or not. To take firm hold of your life, you must first believe that in a free and safe society you alone are the arbiter of your existence.

It may come as a surprise, but the process of taking control of your life not only changes your behaviors, it also changes the way you are in all of your relationships. Some people will applaud you for the courage you have taken to change your life. Others however will hate you for it. It may become necessary to change the boundaries you've established with others. It may have to tell a parent or close friend that you will make your own decisions about things from now on; about what you will do or with whom you will associate. You may have to tell them that you no longer want to do the things you used to do or that you used to allow. You may have to tell an over-protective spouse or parent that you are now in control of your life and that you intend to make decisions that will ultimately make your life better.

3. Develop persistence. It is the only way to be sure that you will get what you want.

Know what you want out of life and insist on getting it. Persistence means never giving up or allowing your self to fall prey to the whims and wants of others. Persistence is refusing to allow obstacles to determine your fate. It also means figuring things out, being a creative problem solver, and staying on your own path no matter what. In Shakespeare's Hamlet, the character Polonius says, "This above all: to thine own self be true, and it must follow, as the night the day, Thou canst not then be false to any man."

You must be true to the path you have chosen because when you do, you are true to yourself. Persistence will not allow you to engage in self-deception—pretending that what you want is not important. Any lack of persistence will allow the enemies of your life to stand between you and any noteworthy achievement you want to make. Don't allow that to happen. Remember, your worst enemies—those within and without—can be defeated once and for all by relentlessly, tenaciously, and repeatedly calling on your courage and forever following through.

4. Learn to ignore criticism

If you can't ignore it, "fake until you make it." Pretend criticism and negativity don't affect you, and soon the practice will become a habit. Close your mind tightly against the negative influences of others including relatives, friends and acquaintances. Your spirit can only work in an attitude of goodness and positivity.

5. Live your life to the fullest

The happy truth is that we can all live our lives any way we choose, however, there is one small uncomfortable caveat we only get to live once. The value of living a satisfying life is not dependent on how long you live but rather how well you have lived.

6. Enlist the power of your spiritual presence

We all have within us a special spiritual essence that emanates from us signaling our presence to those we meet. We have within us the power to cultivate a presence so strong that it touches everyone with whom we come into contact conveying exactly who you are. Even people who believe they aren't spiritual admit they have felt a particular presence from people they didn't know. Some people command respect or attention just by coming into a room. Their spiritual presence precedes them. Sometimes it is possible to feel a sense of wellbeing or trust from people as they come into a room. You too have a spiritual presence and what we believe about ourselves affects that presence.

7. Recognize there is life after failure

Failure is devastating. It feels as though a part of you has been injured. But, don't let yourself be discouraged. Failure doesn't last and recovering from it will take practice. It is only a mindset and apart from the fact that it doesn't feel good, it is the best learning you can experience. Remember, "no failure, no growth."

Marcus Aurelius once asked, "Does what has happened keep you from acting with justice, generosity, self-control, sanity, prudence, honesty, humility, straightforwardness, and all other qualities that allow a person's nature to fulfill itself? So, remember this principle when something threatens to cause you pain: the thing itself was no misfortune at all; to endure it and prevail is great good fortune."

107

8. Do nothing when you're angry.

Anger clouds clear thinking. It tends to submit to commands of emotional behaviors. Do nothing. Wait. Time allows anger to cool. Anger is a response to inner fear and prevents you from seeing what you really want or need. Concentrate on calming yourself both inside and out. Breathe deeply, lower your heart rate, and relax your mind and thoughts. Reacting without focus puts you life-goals at risk. It has the potential of killing important relationships or opportunities. You may say things you don't mean and can't take back.

9. Do nothing when you're feeling insecure.

Feelings of insecurity and uncertainty are a reaction to unrealistic fears. When you are stricken with such feelings, sit and do nothing. Enlist your imagination and reacquaint yourself with your dreams and visions of your anticipated future. Ninety-nine percent of what you fear will never happen.

Take time to occupy your mind with beautiful thoughts while fighting every negative impression. Buy yourself a bunch of flowers, walk in the park, or treat yourself to a shopping spree. God has given everyone the strength of will and the capacity to control your thinking; use them both.

10. Do nothing when you are feeling frantic.

Stop. Just stop dead in your tracks—stop moving, thinking, or engaging. Busy activities and frantic thinking fuels frenzied emotions. Break the cycle of frantic worry by engaging in calming behaviors: Read a book. Write. Take a shower. Take a walk. In short, sit and do absolutely nothing. Once you are calm, you can take life on again. It's when we are in touch with the magic of silence that we are able to come in contact with your inner peace.

11. Do nothing when you're anxious or worried.

There is nothing that is so important that it can't wait. The idea that any situation carries with it a time factor is often unlikely. It's tough to be productive in your daily life when anxiety and worry dominate your thoughts. Anxiety and worry are the result of feelings of powerlessness. They are fueled by thoughts and beliefs that may or may not be true. Instead of engaging anxious thoughts, tell yourself you are going to stop worrying for now. If you have to, create a "worry time." where you will worry for only 30 minutes and no longer. Then, during that time, go over your worry list and zero in on all those things that aren't worry worthy; most of what we worry about never ever happens and doesn't actually exists. Put worry on notice that it is not going to control your life. After all, why would any one allow something that will never happen to have so much authority over their lives?

12. Do nothing when you're tired.

You can't think clearly when you are tired and judgment is impaired. Sleep deprivation causes forgetfulness, pessimism, sadness, stress, and powers anger. Often when someone is in a bad mood, they are merely just tired. A lack or sleep or scheduled relaxation affects your ability to solve even small daily problems or complete uncomplicated tasks. Do nothing until you are rested and reinvigorated.

13. Do nothing when you want to be liked

You should do nothing when you realize that you are behaving just so someone will like you; mother, a boss, a friend, a stranger, etc. Do nothing if it appears you are behaving to obtain praise, flattery, love, or to avoid neglect. None of these things are real if you must do something to get them. It is an illusion for which you are failing to recognize reality.

14. Display your brilliance: Be the 'you' you were always meant to be

All through this book we have been uncovering the essential pillars that hold up the principles necessary for making strength-based decisions. In chapter one, we explained that it is never your circumstance that defines who you are; it is the choices you have made throughout your life and continue to make.

Throughout Decision we have been laying out the guidelines indispensible to making strength-based decisions—decisions in keeping with who you are and what you want in this life. Choices made with power, focus, and clarity reflect who you are and alter the direction of your life with new promise. It prompts newly evolved creativity, imagination, and an inspiration that commands your inner brilliance to show its self.

We have already discussed the importance of being self-aware and learning your particular needs, wants, likes, dislikes, talents, and skills.

Once you have incorporated all the pillars of strength-based decision-making simultaneously and practiced each principle, you will become the person you have always been but may not have had the courage to acknowledge. You are brilliant, just as gold, silver, and diamonds are brilliant. You were created to achieve great things, so dream dreams that are big enough to be worthy of who you are. Give your dreams the focused time and attention that you give other important things in your life and you will be surprised by the wonderful successes you will experience. Focus on your strengths and be determined to let the brilliance within you shine. Do what you do best. Become the vision you have always held for yourself. Focus your thinking, be suspicious of negative influences, and take on those opportunities God has planned for you. Don't bother to ask yourself if you can do this or that. Only ask yourself when and how you will do it, and the brilliance that is within you will supply the answer. When you make conscientious decisions from a position of power—decisions that reflect who you are and change the direction of your life—you will automatically allow your brilliance to become known.

Once you acknowledge the enormity of who you are, you can begin to work on your dreams with decisiveness, conviction, and concentration. You can move forward with confidence without second-guessing yourself or belittling yourself for the thought.

You have a unique light to share with the world, as well as, an important way of being that will influence your life and the lives of others for good. Go for it.

PILLAR REFLECTION SECTION: THE DISCERNMENT TRIAD

When its decision time ignorance is not bless. What filters did you fail to use?

_____

_____

_____

_____

_____

_____

_____

_____

_____

_____

_____

_____

Pillar Action Section: The Discernment Triad

Discernment requires faith, time and recognition. Given the time and faith you will learn to make the right decision for you. What would that look like?

_____

_____

_____

_____

_____

_____

_____

_____

_____

_____

_____

_____

_____

Please bring your questions about this pillar to Decision Time live event or a complimentary call with Stone Love.

_____

_____

_____

_____

_____

_____

_____

_____

_____

_____

_____

NOTES

The End

ABOUT THE AUTHOR

Stone Love Founder of Stoneologys, Author Speaker, and Mentor

Stone Love, has been introduced as, "A Light" She defines herself as a mentor with experiential wisdom. Her wisdom gained through choices for self-love, making strength-based decisions and nurturing relationships.

Stone is a devoted wife and mother of 5 daughters and a son. Stone is also a grandmother of 15.

Stone's rock of 25 years 'Mr. Fauréal'

My mom's legacy of love continues with her grands.

I can see her in the eyes of each of our grandchildren.

Grands Grandmom, Granddad, & Grandpa

She is the Founder of Stoneologys and originator of The 7 Pillars of Strength-Based Decision Making. I've talked to thousands of women around the world about the decision making process. During my research, I found the number one thing preventing us from reaching our full potential is the inability to make strength-based decisions. I've collected data from women in Southern Caribbean, Costa Rica, Haiti, and throughout the United States, and Canada. The answer is always the same; it is our decisions, not our circumstance that defines the quality of our lives.

Decision Time is written to give readers a comprehensive, step-by-step process for making the right decision in every situation, every time. The principles that Decision Time outlines prove that there is no need to ever grapple with uncertainty again. It teaches how to navigate a landscape of multiple options in a sea of choices by understanding yourself and knowing what you really want. It is a book designed to help you ascertain what your deep-seated objectives are. It defines what conscious and unconscious influencers are operating in each decision. Reflection of the impact of poor thinking habits, unconscious repetitive behaviors, and the disregard of intuition leads to poor decisions.

It is possible to get what you want, be who you are, and make decisions that serve the direction you want your life to go. Join the thousands of others who have redirected their lives by employing the power of strength-based decision-making."

Stone spent 100 hours leaning from Oprah Winfrey and her 'Trail blazers,' Deepak Chopra, Iyanla Vanzant and Rob Bell. She shares this philosophy with Oprah,

"Every moment you have the choice to open up...to listen to the whisper and live the way your life is nudging you to live...to walk boldly on your own life's path."

~ Oprah Winfrey

Photo Credit: Live The Life You Love

Stone attended Tony Robbins 5 day event in New Jersey. Learning how to control her state of mind and take action in spite of the fear, she determined to successfully conquer the 'Fire Walk'. Stone has walked through the fire spiritually, so on the physical plane she knows she can do anything.

Mrs. Love's experiential wisdom is a combination of experience, intuition and the desire to course correct life's set backs. She has dedicated her professional life to mentoring, inspiring and empowering professional women and young girls to intuitively turn their life lessons into blessings. Speaking and training internationally, Stone also uses social media to engage online communities that enable people all over the world to follow in that mission.

Stone discovered that many, if not most women were habitually making decisions based on low self-esteem and the secrecy of childhood sexual abuse.

Stone originated, a process that begins to redirect lessons into the blessing. Therefore, making a 'Strength-Based Decision' every time.

Stone knows that sharing the benefits of experience will prevent procrastination and limited visions in women. Stone has the made the correlation between the shame and guilt of childhood sexual abuse, and poor choices and decisions made as an adult. By studying the brilliance in a resilient spirit.

Offering mentoring and inspirational programs both live and virtual. The main conversation is not about the gory details of abuse, rather we place the power in understanding manipulation so that we can prevent it before it manifest. Together we create a path to our intuitive strengths through learning the 7 Pillars of Strength-Based Decision making.

To learn more please visit:
www.stoneologys.com

Bring these questions or comments to the next Courage2Decide workshop or join us on our C2D Private Community where we are changing lives one decision at a time.

_____

_____

_____

_____

_____

_____

_____

_____

_____

_____

_____

_____

For booking information please visit:
www.stonelovespeakerspage.com

To schedule a 'Decision Time' Book Signing & Workshop for
your group of women or young girls, go to
DecisionTimeBookTalk.com

**To be apart of the Stoneologys community and receive your
Decision Time workbook please visit:** courage2decide.com
and sign up to receive notifications of workshops and events
across the country.

To attend a Courage2Decide workshop please visit:
www.courage2decide.com events page to register.

**For coaching and mentoring programs please send your
email** request to: **stonelove@stoneologys.com**